QUICK SKILLS

WRITING IN THE WORKPLACE

Marylyn E. Calabrese, Ph.D.
Career Solutions Training Group
Paoli, PA

VISIT US ON THE INTERNET
www.swep.com
www.thomson.com

South-Western
Thomson Learning™

Cincinnati • Albany, NY • Belmont, CA • Bonn • Boston • Detroit • Johannesburg • London • Madrid
Melbourne • Mexico City • New York • Paris • Singapore • Tokyo • Toronto • Washington

Peter McBride: Business Unit Director
Eve Lewis: Team Leader
Laurie Wendell: Project Manager
Alan Biondi: Editor
Patricia Matthews Boies: Production Manager
Kathy Hampton: Manufacturing Coordinator
Mark Linton: Marketing Manager
Linda Wasserman: Marketing Coordinator

Thanks to the following educators and trainers
who provided valuable assistance during the development of the QUICK SKILLS materials:

Robert W. Moses
Vice President for Planning and Program Development
Indian River Community College
Fort Pierce, Florida

Richard Winn
Director, Educational Projects
Heald Colleges
San Francisco, California

Debra Mills
Education-to-Careers/Tech Prep Director
Danville Area Community College
Danville, Illinois

Patrick Highland
Director of Vocational Education
Iowa City Community School District
Iowa City, Iowa

Julie Kibler
Business Teacher and Business Department Chairperson
Castle High School
Newburgh, Indiana

Dave Hyslop
External Liaison
Bowling Green State University
Bowling Green, Ohio

Dr. Doris Humphrey: Project Manager
Jane Galli: Production Editor
Pam Dooley: Typography

13 East Central Avenue, Paoli, PA 19301
Telephone: 1-888-299-2784 • FAX: (610) 993-8249
E-mail: cstg@bellatlantic.net • Website: www.careersolutionsgroup.com

CONTENTS

Today's companies depend on information to maintain their competitive edge, and that means most employees have to write. Gone is the day when a mechanic needed only the skill to repair a broken motor and a horticulturist needed only the expertise to grow healthy plants. Workers now fill out forms, request information, compose memos, file reports, and use e-mail. Some take notes in meetings, send faxes, draft reports, write proposals, and respond to customer requests. They also write newsletters, operation manuals, and new product descriptions. Ask any of the employees described below if they expected writing to be such a key element of their job and you'll get a resounding "no."

- Ty, a physical therapy assistant, prepares reports about the treatment he provides and each patient's response to the treatment.
- Carla, who is a police officer, fills out incident reports every day.
- When Ahmed, a legal assistant, approaches his boss with an idea for the employee newsletter, he is asked to submit a rough draft.
- Kim, who's preparing for a career as a machinist, serves on the advisory board of her training program and writes reports for other trainees to study.

- The messages that Deirdre—a telephone receptionist—takes are often long and involved and have to be written clearly and concisely.
- Pierre works as a summer intern for a financial institution; he has to write goals and objectives for each project he does.

Writers make decisions about whom to write, what to say, and in what format to say it. In other words, they make decisions about purpose, audience, and format—the key elements of workplace writing. The *purpose* of a business document determines what is written. The *audience*—or *reader*—establishes how it is written, and the *format* presents it in a reader-friendly manner. In the first two workshops of this book, you will learn about purpose, and in Workshop 3 you'll focus on the reader and audience. Workshop 4 shows you how to organize the content and is followed by Workshop 5, which features language techniques. In Workshop 6, you'll learn how to avoid annoying errors; and in Workshop 7, you'll learn about different types of business documents. The Revising Guidelines on page 91 will be especially helpful as you develop your writing skills.

The following self assessment will help you evaluate your writing skills. Many of the items refer to common misconceptions about work-related writing and all are discussed in the workshops.

Are these statements true or false? Circle T or F to indicate your answer.

1.	Good writing uses big words and long sentences.	T	F
2.	Experienced writers always make an outline before they begin to write.	T	F
3.	Revising a document usually means checking for spelling and punctuation errors.	T	F
4.	Unclear wording and poor organization are two common problems in workplace writing.	T	F
5.	Learning the rules of grammar is the best way to improve your writing.	T	F
6.	Experienced writers rarely revise; inexperienced writers revise a lot.	T	F
7.	Errors in spelling, punctuation, and grammar usage can distract the reader from the meaning of a document.	T	F
8.	It's important to get most of your thoughts down on paper before rereading and revising.	T	F
9.	Reading the daily newspaper on a regular basis can help you improve your writing.	T	F
10.	In asking for feedback from others on your writing, ask for a specific response, not general reactions.	T	F

Answers: 1. F; 2. F; 3. F; 4. T; 5. F; 6. F; 7. T; 8. T; 9. T; 10. T.

How did you do on your self-assessment? If you gave a few wrong answers, don't worry; the upcoming workshops will help you become a better writer. Let's get started.

Carmen is applying for a position as an animal caretaker at the local zoo. Since she was a small child, she has dreamed of a career working with animals. This job blends perfectly with her interest in biology and is excellent training for

her long-term goal as zookeeper, the top management job. She knows she'll have to attend graduate school, complete a lengthy internship, and add several years' experience before she is ready for the top job, but this is a great start.

She loves animals, is a responsible worker, comes to work every day, takes instructions well, listens carefully, gets along with people, and never considers a task too large or small. A former employer, a veterinarian, who says Carmen's best quality is her positive attitude, has volunteered to serve as a reference.

The zoo's human resource manager told Carmen that everyone applying for the job must send a cover letter and a resumé. The selection of interviewees will come from these written documents.

Carmen knows her purpose in writing will be to describe why she would be a good animal caretaker. Explaining her background is easy in a one-on-one conversation, but reducing it to a few good sentences will be a challenge.

What's Inside

In these pages, you will learn to:

Identify the Purpose

All workplace documents, actually all types of writing, have a purpose; and you should think about the purpose before you start. If you're not certain what you want to say, just begin. The act of writing will help you discover and clarify your purpose.

What the reader needs to know determines the purpose of a document. For Carmen, the purpose of her cover letter is to get an interview. If she describes adequately to the human resources manager why she will be a good caretaker, she will almost certainly be invited for an interview.

In the workplace, people write with one or more of the following purposes in mind. They want to (1) convey information, (2) make requests, (3) persuade, or (4) express goodwill. The best business writers communicate their messages in concise, simple language with a positive, businesslike tone.

This workshop covers the purpose of conveying information. In Workshop 2 you will learn about other purposes.

Reasons for Workplace Writing

Purpose	Method	Examples

Convey information
   inform
   describe
   instruct
   explain
	Tell why you're writing.
	Explain the details (who, what when, where, why, how).
	Restate the most important points.
	Close on a positive note.
		E-mail message describing a problem
		
		Letter answering a request or complaint
		Memo announcing a plan or policy
		Memo explaining how to answer phone calls

Make requests	Tell why you're writing. Provide details. State the action requested. Close on a positive note.	Letter requesting information Letter ordering a product
Persuade	Get the reader's attention. Tell why you're writing. Show how the reader will benefit. Minimize any obstacles for the reader. Use a strong, positive closing.	E-mail message requesting a meeting Resumé cover letter Follow-up letter Sales letter
Express goodwill	Tell why you're writing. Refer to the occasion. Express your sentiments.	Note thanking a co-worker for support Letter thanking customers for their business E-mail message congratulating an associate

Workplace documents are written for different purposes because they answer different needs. Although any document may have more than one purpose, usually one purpose is the most important. Review the purposes described in the following examples:

- A hospital brochure primarily gives information about the hospital's services, but it also communicates goodwill to the community.
- A newspaper advertisement to persuade potential customers to buy sneakers also provides information about the product.
- The message in documents that acknowledge orders, grant requests, extend invitations, approve adjustments, announce meetings, or explain schedule changes is positive or neutral.
- Documents that acknowledge orders alert customers that goods are on their way and also create good will.
- Announcements of schedule changes convey essential information but also show consideration and build employee trust.
- Invitations to company picnics create good will and also develop a sense of community spirit.

Conveying Information

Workplace documents inform their readers by describing, explaining, or instructing. Typical examples include product descriptions, informational brochures, press releases, policy statements, instructional manuals, as well as a variety of office documents like meeting announcements, status reports, conference summaries, e-mail messages, and correspondence.

> " To express the most difficult matters clearly and intelligently is to strike coins out of pure gold. "
>
> — Geibel

Bad (• Putting off till last minute,
• Wait till the end to make changes.

Positive or Neutral Information

In the following e-mail message, the human resources department sends an announcement to all employees who have registered for a workshop the department organized. The purpose is to confirm the registration, give details about the time and place, and welcome participants to the program.

Notice that the first sentence states the purpose clearly and the following sentences list the details the reader needs to know. Because the message is something Alicia Henderson wants to hear, it is placed at the beginning. The last sentence provides a friendly closing.

To: Ahenderson@yorksys.com
From: NevaHusam@yorksys.com
Subject: Document Design Workshop Confirmation

Your registration for the March 6 workshop on document design is confirmed. The meeting will be held in conference room B on the second floor of the Babcock building next to the cafeteria. Please note the workshop schedule. We will begin promptly at 8:30 a.m.

8:30-9:00	Coffee and welcome
9:00-12:00	Morning session
12:00-1:00	Lunch break
1:00-4:00	Afternoon session
4:00-4:15	Wrap up and closing

Because this program will include many opportunities for audience participation, you may wish to bring samples of your documents for evaluation and revision.

I look forward to seeing you on March 6.

If the information you're conveying is positive or neutral, follow these steps:

1. State the purpose first by explaining the good or neutral news. In the first paragraph, tell why you're writing.

    Your registration is confirmed.

2. Supply the relevant details. Explain what the reader needs to know. State all the information clearly and correctly.

    The meeting will be held in conference room B on the second floor of the Babcock building next to the cafeteria. Please note the workshop schedule. We will begin promptly at 8:30 a.m.:

8:30-9:00	*Coffee and welcome*
9:00-12:00	*Morning session*
12:00-1:00	*Lunch break*
1:00-4:00	*Afternoon session*
4:00-4:15	*Wrap-up and closing*

Because this program will include many opportunities for audience participation, you may wish to bring samples of your documents for evaluation and revision.

3. Close on a positive note. End every message in a cordial manner.

    I look forward to seeing you on March 6.

Positive or neutral messages are direct, straightforward, and usually easy to write. Readers like to receive these types of messages. Use your positive or neutral message opportunities to practice writing clearly, simply, and concisely. Once you have decided on the main point or purpose, use the rest of the message for any other important details.

> Good writing is clear thinking made visible.
>
> — Bill Wheeler

Watch for Snow

Recent snowstorms have caused changes in your department's regular schedule. Send an e-mail message to all department members announcing that the Friday meeting is postponed and rescheduled for the following Friday. Follow the steps listed on the previous page.

To: Transdept@isu.com

From: Dsagiotes@isu.com

Subject: January 6 Meeting Rescheduled

_____

_____

_____

_____

_____

_____

_____

_____

_____

_____

_____

_____

Conveying Negative Information

Messages that refuse a request, deny credit, cancel a program, or tell a customer an order will be delayed convey bad news. The strategy for writing a bad news message is more involved than the strategy for writing a good or neutral news message, but even negative information can be presented in a positive way.

When the purpose of writing is to convey negative information, the document should begin with a positive or neutral comment—often called a "buffer," such as, "Thank you for your request." The purpose of a buffer is to be polite, but not to mislead the reader. Be careful not to cross the line between these two.

In the following e-mail message, Jamika Owings learns that she cannot take the workshop on document design.

To: Jowings@yorksys.com
From: NevaHusam@yorksys.com
Subject: Registration for Document Design Workshop

Thank you for registering for the March 6 workshop on document design. I appreciate your interest in our programs.

This workshop—our most popular program—was filled within one week of its announcement, and your registration arrived after all seats were taken. To accommodate the many requests for this program, we are scheduling an additional session on April 17.

Please let me know if you would like to register for that date.

> " The secret of good writing is to say an old thing in a new way or to say a new thing in an old way. "
>
> —— Edward G. Bulwer-Lyon

If the information you are conveying is negative, follow these steps.

1. Begin with a neutral or pleasant statement. This prepares the reader for the rest of the message.

   Thank you for registering for the March 6 workshop on document design. I appreciate your interest in our programs.

2. Explain the reason for the refusal. Providing background information helps the reader understand and accept the bad news.

   This workshop—our most popular program—was filled within one week of its announcement, and your registration arrived after all seats were taken.

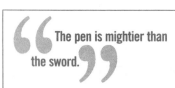

3. State or imply the refusal. Try to state the bad news in a positive or a neutral way. Almost any bad news can be conveyed in a manner that reduces a reader's negative reaction, usually offering a practical reason for the bad news is the best approach.

   your registration arrived after all seats were taken

4. Offer an alternative, if possible. Suggesting other options is good business. Often, the reader will be equally or more pleased with the option.

   To accommodate the many requests for this program, we are scheduling an additional session on April 17.

   End on a positive note. Positive endings can make a reader feel better, even if the news is bad. The best writers are able to build good will, even when the message is negative, by focusing on a point that allows the reader to take positive action in return.

   Please let me know if you would like to register for that date.

> **"The pen is mightier than the sword."**
> — Edward Bulwer Lytton

Deliver Bad News

You work in the office of a photographer who specializes in family portraits. When a mix-up occurs, three proofs are sent to the wrong family. Write a note to Mario Esposa explaining that his complete order will be delayed one week. Do not go into detail about the mix-up because the loss of privacy could anger Mr. Esposa. Explain only that his pictures are delayed because of a processing error. Follow the guidelines for documents that deliver bad news.

Family Fotos
56 Line Road
Meriden, CT

Mario Esposa
456 Alagon Drive
Stillwater, OK 74078

Dear Mr. Esposa:

_____

_____

_____

_____

_____

_____

_____

_____

_____

_____

_____

Sincerely,

_____

Your Name
Family Fotos

GETTING CONNECTED

Many websites have resources for writers. Log on to the Internet and connect to two comprehensive ones with help on a variety of topics.

"Resources for Writers and Writing Instructors" by Jack Lynch at Rutgers University

http://andromeda.rutgers.edu/~jlynch/Writing/links.html

and "Garbl's Writing Resources Online"

www.garbl.com

Click on "active writing" for help with defining the purpose of a document.

WORKSHOP WRAP-UP

- Workplace writers make decisions about purpose for every document they write.
- A writer determines the purpose of a document by assessing what the reader needs to know or do.
- Workplace documents that convey information include product descriptions, policy statements, instructional manuals, informational brochures, status reports, employee newsletters, office correspondence, and e-mail.
- Writers use different techniques to convey positive or neutral information and to convey negative information.

Manuel knows that it will be hard for him to get time off without giving several weeks' notice. But he wants to take some vacation days to be with his best friend, Juan, from Guatemala.

When Juan called last night to say he would be in the United States in three weeks, he and Manuel spent over an hour talking about all the sights they would see and trips they would take. At the time, being gone from work for a few days didn't seem like such a big deal to Manuel; but this morning he's having second thoughts about asking his boss for a vacation.

Company policy says all unusual requests have to be made in writing with specific reasons for the request. Persuading his supervisor to let him take a week's vacation on short notice will be tough, and Manuel hardly knows where to begin.

The first thing he decides to do is come up with a good opening—one that will gets his supervisor's attention. "Maybe," Manuel thinks, "I will just say something about my friend visiting from another country, but that doesn't sound like an important enough reason."

As Manuel continues to think about his persuasive message, he decides the hardest part will be showing some benefit to the reader, his boss. How can his friend's visit possibly be helpful to the company? Manuel decides to wait until tonight, call Juan back, and develop a strategy for the letter.

What's Inside

Direct Requests

Many workplace documents make direct requests, for such items as general information, customer service, or product details. For example, a letter might request one of the following:

"Please send me a copy of your latest catalog."

"Can you come to a meeting next Tuesday at 2 p.m.?

"Please send me these items advertised in your September circular."

In the following letter, Loc Nguyen places an order for a CD that will help him in his training program as a manufacturing specialist. Note his use of specific details. His request is simple, straightforward, and complete.

> " All words are pegs to hang ideas on. "
>
> —— Henry Ward Beecher

Alleghany Technical Institute
90 Broadway
Atlanta, Georgia 30303

December 18, 20xx

Charlotte Bangor
Technical Support Products
13 East Central Avenue
Nashville, TN 37312

Dear Ms. Banger:
This is my order for the two videotapes listed below. I do not have an order form.

- *Tips for the New Manufacturing Specialist*
- *Turning Your Job Into A Career*

The ad stated that each video tape costs $169, which includes shipping and handling. Please charge this amount to my StartSmart account as follows:
Loc Nguyen
Account Number: 38539 000 1234 0000
Expiration date: 11/20xx

Sincerely,

Loc Nguyen

Follow the steps below to write a direct request.

1. **Summarize your request.** Explain why you are writing. Ask a question or state a purpose.

   This is my order for the two videotapes listed below. I do not have an order form.

2. **Provide all the necessary details.** Anticipate and answer any questions the reader may have about your request.

Tips for the New Manufacturing Specialist Turning Your Job Into a Career

3. **Tell the reader exactly what to do.** Explain any items that could be confusing.

   Please charge this amount to my StartSmart account as follows:
   Loc Nguyen
   Account Number: 38539 000 1234 0000
   Expiration date: 11/20xx

ACTIVITY 2.1

Ask for a Reference

Most job applications ask you to list three or more references from people who can describe your work habits, reliability, and skills in doing the job. You should always ask permission before using anyone as a reference. Follow the guidelines above for making requests, then use the space below to request permission from a former employer or teacher to be used as a reference.

_____
Date

_____
Name
_____
Street Address
_____
City, State, Zip

Dear _____

_____

_____

_____

_____

Sincerely,

Your Name

Documents That Persuade

The purpose of many documents is to persuade. A persuasive message tries to get the reader to take an action, such as hiring, purchasing, or donating money.

You've probably sent and received many messages like these. They include brochures, proposals, requests for job interviews, promotional sales letters, pleas for charitable donations, and requests for political endorsements.

Manuel needed to write a persuasive letter to his supervisor about taking vacation days to spend time with his friend. This letter will be harder to write than a direct request because Manuel

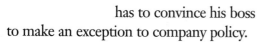

has to convince his boss to make an exception to company policy.

Persuasive messages are similar to request messages in that both ask the reader to do something. A persuasive message, however, starts with a bold statement that gets the reader's attention, then lists the benefits to the reader for acting. In the following letter, Jason Wilensky demonstrates how to write a letter that persuades.

Read Jason's letter and decide whether he followed the guidelines for writing persuasive letters.

Jason worked for many years after he left high school. Now he is enrolled in a technical institute, training to become a printing press operator. To fulfill his program's internship requirement, he has to persuade a local print shop to mentor him one morning a week. When Jason visited a printer in his neighborhood whom he has known for many years, he was asked to submit a letter describing his qualifications.

> Like stones, words are laborious and unforgiving, and the fitting of them together, like the fitting of stones, demands great patience, strength of purpose, and skill.
>
> — Edmund Morrison

456 Center Street
Thompson City, NM 87662

November 21, 20xx

Mr. Marco DeAngelo
333 Market Street
Thompson City, NM 87662

Dear Mr. DeAngelo:

Remember the many times I visited your print shop and asked if I could help? You always told me to come back when I was older, when I was ready to pitch in and really work. Well, I'm ready now.

This spring will be my last quarter at the Turner Technical Institute, where I'm completing a certificate program in printing press operation. One of the requirements is the fulfillment of a one-morning-a week internship for about 14 weeks. Would you please sponsor me for that internship?

Ever since I was a kid, I have enjoyed everything about the printing business—talking to customers, planning each job, designing the page layout, and most of all, creating the finished product—whether a one-page flyer or a multi-page book. Here are my qualifications:

- Successful completion of all required courses at Turner Technical Institute, including Fundamentals of Printing, Pagemaker, Photoshop, and Quark Express
- Experience in the school's print shop on different types of printing machines
- Enthusiasm and love of the printing industry
- Willingness to learn and benefit from the on-the-job training that an operation like yours can provide

You'll be pleased you decided to mentor me. I promise to work hard, listen carefully, and follow instructions. You won't have to ask me twice to follow through on an assignment.

My resumé is attached. Next week, I'll call to ask for an appointment. I will enjoy talking with you again.

Sincerely,

Jason Wilensky

Jason received an appointment. His letter fulfills all the requirements for a document that persuades. When the purpose is to persuade, follow these steps:

1. **Get the reader's attention.** Start with a question, an interesting fact, or a mutual interest.

Remember the many times I visited your print shop and asked if I could help?

2. **State the purpose.** Ask for what you want—clearly and directly.

You always told me to come back when I was older, when I was ready to pitch in and really work. Well, I'm ready now.

3. **Show the benefits to the reader.** Provide evidence and details that will make your case.

Ever since I was a kid, I have enjoyed everything about the printing business—talking to customers, planning each job, designing the page layout, and most of all, creating the finished product, whether it is a one-page flyer or a multi-page book.

Here are my qualifications:

- *Successful completion of all required courses at Turner Technical Institute, including Fundamentals of Printing, Pagemaker, Photoshop, and Quark Express.*
- *Experience in the school's print shop on different types of printing machines.*
- *Enthusiasm and love of the printing industry.*
- *Willingness to learn and benefit from the on-the-job training that an operation like yours can provide.*

4. **Minimize any obstacles the reader may have.** Anticipate and respond to any possible objections.

You'll be pleased you decided to mentor me. I promise to work hard, listen carefully, and follow instructions. You won't have to ask me twice to follow through on an assignment.

5. **Use a strong goodwill closing.** Restate your request and tell how you will follow up.

My resumé is attached. Next week, I'll call to ask for an appointment. I will enjoy talking with you again.

What's Your Point?

You serve on a company committee that arranges sports and social activities. Although you usually play a major role in planning the spring picnic, your work schedule for the next quarter will be unusually heavy. You want to stay on the committee and help with the picnic, but you cannot take on any major responsibilities as you have in the past. You need to make the point clear in a memo to the other committee members.

Write one sentence that states the purpose of your message. Then follow up with several sentences of supporting details that clarify the message.

To: Social Committee Members

From: _____
           Your name

Date: _____

Subject: Assistance on the Committee

Purpose: _____

_____

_____

_____

_____

_____

Supporting details: _____

_____

_____

_____

_____

_____

_____

Expressing Goodwill

All workplace writing should be positive and businesslike, but some messages, such as letters of congratulations and invitations, are written for the sole purpose of expressing good will. Goodwill documents also show appreciation and recognition, offer congratulations on outstanding achievements, and say thank you. Building relationships through goodwill letters can help you in your work and career and is a powerful reason for writing.

♦ Lucas Watts, a draftsman for a tool manufacturer, sends a goodwill message to thank his employer for allowing him to take time off to attend a cousin's wedding in another state. He wants to tell his employer how much he appreciates this extra consideration.

Read the letter he wrote. Notice that this letter is short, specific, and upbeat.

Thank you messages are not difficult to write, and they usually impress the people who receive them. Even more important, thank you messages are good business.

May 3, 20xx

Mr. Andreas Gabe
Market Masters
603 Latham Lane
Aldline, FL 30

Dear Mr. Phillips:

Thank you for granting me the opportunity to attend my cousin Letitia's wedding in California. My presence was very important to my aunt and uncle, whom I hadn't seen in several years.

It is nice to work for a company where family requests are important.

Sincerely,

Luther Watts

> **Letters are among the most significant memorial a person can leave behind.**
>
> — Johann Wolfgang Von Goethe

I Appreciate Your Business.

As a salesperson in a children's clothing store, one of your tasks is to write letters of appreciation to customers who make large purchases. You always include a $25 store coupon. On a recent visit to your store, Bill Marzolf spent $2000 on spring clothes for his five grandchildren.

Complete the note below by inviting Mr. Marzolf to return to the store and use the enclosed coupon. Add other details as appropriate. You can describe the new fall clothes and note when they will be arriving or say something about the grandchildren. The store wants this customer to come back.

The Children's Place
Central City, NH 03772

April 23, 20xx

Mr. B. Marzolf
89 North Main Avenue
Hyde Park, NH 03772

Dear Mr. Marzolf:

_____

_____

_____

_____

_____

_____

_____

Sincerely,

Your name, Sales Associate

Why Are You Writing?

The writer, the type of document, and the intended reader are listed in columns 1, 2, and 3 of the chart below. Fill in columns 4 and 5 to explain why each document might have been written. You should make up your answers to fit the situation. For example, a public health officer might write a brochure for the general purpose of conveying information and the specific purpose of describing the symptoms of Lyme disease. As you complete this chart, you will notice the purpose that dominates most business writing is conveying information.

Job title	Document	Reader	General Purpose	Specific Purpose
public health officer	brochure	public	convey information	describe symptoms of Lyme disease
accounting clerk	status memo	accounting manager	convey information	notify past due accounts
awning salesperson	letter	potential customers	persuade	sell awnings
chef	letter	vendor	request	order new equipment
preschool aide	letter	parents	express goodwill	note child's good progress
shop steward	memo	supervisor	_____	_____
lab assistant	monthly report	lab director	_____	_____
secretary	meeting notes	boss	_____	_____
computer software specialist	memo	client	_____	_____
paralegal	e-mail	attorneys in firm	_____	_____
job seeker	cover letter to potential employer		_____	_____
pest control technician	status report to supervisor		_____	_____

Clarify Your Purpose

Once you identify the purpose of your message, you must make the purpose obvious to the reader. Unless the reader understands clearly, the message may go unread and unanswered. Here are ways to ensure that your message is read.

1. *Before you write.* If you're having difficulty deciding why you are writing, try writing your purpose in a sentence of 15 or fewer words. Although you may not actually use this sentence in your document, the strategy will help you focus on what is important.

2. *After you write.* Reread the document quickly. Skim the sentence, then ask yourself, "what's the purpose?" If you can't come up with an *immediate* and *simple* response, go back and rethink what you're trying to say. Rewrite the sentence if necessary.

Remember that most documents begin with a statement of the purpose.

Exceptions include bad news messages, which begin with a positive or neutral statement and persuasive messages, which get the reader's attention before the purpose is stated.

GETTING CONNECTED

One of the best websites for writing resources is the Writing Center at Purdue University.

http://owl.english.purdue.edu/

For additional suggestions on getting your purpose across in writing, log on to this website. Click on "Resources for Writers," then go to "Instructional Index of Handouts and find the one called "Planning/when you start to write," Or click on "Professional Writing," and then go to the subtopic on persuasion.

WORKSHOP WRAP-UP

- Workplace documents that persuade or request action include proposals, requests for payment, cover letters that accompany resumés, sales brochures, fundraising letters,and direct mail advertising.
- Workplace documents that communicate goodwill include letters of congratulations, customer appreciation notices, and a variety of thank-you notes to readers inside and outside the company.
- Writers use different techniques to assure that their documents convey a clear purpose.

3 WORKSHOP

Tyrone is the purchasing agent for a small, urban school district. Each spring he sends a letter and a purchasing request form to all staff members asking them to identify their equipment and supplies needs for the upcoming school year. Although he allows two months for a response, many people miss the deadline; and those who do reply on time often do not return complete information, omitting such essentials as the product number, the preferred supplier, number of items requested, and costs.

In the days preceding this year's deadline, Tyrone's office is plagued with telephone callers asking for assistance in completing the form. Finally, one staff member blurts out in frustration, "We don't understand what you want! Please explain."

After reviewing his letter and form, Tyrone sees that both are unclear and vague. When he used the words "identify supplies and equipment," he assumed incorrectly that the staff would know that he needed concrete, precise descriptions, such as:

- AX432876PO, one 6'x8' pine table, Essex Manufacturing, $489
- P8374-34, 50 reams of 8 1/2" x 11" white 20-lb. copier paper, Whitfield Paper Products, @2.89 per ream
- P434-3875, one open-front, 5-shelf laminated pine cabinet, Marshall Cabinetry, $329

Instead, he received descriptions that read, "a table to display lab projects for my science room," "paper for the copier," and "a big cabinet for storing books."

Tyrone recognizes that what he knows about ordering requirements and what the staff knows are different. If he had written the letter to a group of purchase agents, they would have filled out the form completely; but since he wrote to people who order infrequently, he needed to write to their level of understanding.

What's Inside

In these pages, you will learn to:

> " One of the most serious problems in business writing today is not grammatical mistakes, not proofreading errors, but writing that ignores the reader. "
>
> — Anonymous

Identifying the Reader

After determining the purpose of your documents, the next step is to identify the reader. Workplace readers include customers or clients, supervisors and subordinates, co-workers and peers, suppliers, and the larger public. All of these people have different interests, backgrounds, and levels of understanding about your subject.

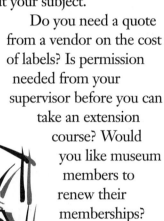

Do you need a quote from a vendor on the cost of labels? Is permission needed from your supervisor before you can take an extension course? Would you like museum members to renew their memberships? You will approach these readers differently, so you should find out as much as you can about each one before you write the first word. Answer the following questions before you begin writing and your task will be easier.

1. What will motivate the recipient to read what I have to say?
2. What is the reader's age? Does age influence how this particular message will be received?
3. What is the socioeconomic status of the reader? Is it a factor in my message?
4. What is the ethnic background of the reader? For this document, does ethnic background matter?
5. Is the reader highly knowledgeable or not knowledgeable at all about my subject?
6. Is the reader male or female? For this message, does gender matter?
7. What is the reader's political affiliation? Is political bias a factor to be considered?

Identify the Approach

The reader's background affects the approach a writer takes in a document. For example, a recreation department director who wants a budget approved would probably write the proposal for her boss differently than she would a press release about a new intergenerational program for teenagers and senior citizens. Here are some questions you can ask when analyzing your audience:

1. How will the reader react to my message?
2. How can I decrease the possibility of a negative reaction?
3. What information does the reader need in order to respond positively to my request?
4. How will the reader use the document?
5. What kind of language or format does the reader expect?
6. Is this message important to the reader? If so, why? If not, why not?

Answers to these questions will determine the content and presentation of your message.

ACTIVITY 3.1

What Do You Want to Know?

Several writers are identified below. If you were writing to their audience for them, what two things would you want to know?

A veterinarian plans to write an instruction sheet about the care and handling of pets.

1. _____

2. _____

A computer salesperson plans to write small business owners about the features of the software program she sells.

1. _____

2. _____

A park ranger is asked to write one page to give to visitors about the uniqueness of the park.

1. _____

2. _____

A consultant plans to write a proposal to develop a new work contract with some of his past clients.

1. _____

2. _____

Use a You Attitude

With more and more information being generated and received by computers, FAX machines, and other electronic equipment, the human element of messages often gets overlooked. Readers forget that messages they receive were written by people, and writers forget they are writing to people.

The most effective workplace documents address a specific audience. Writers of these documents cannot see their readers' faces as they would in a conversation, so they imagine their audience and write from the point of view of the reader.

When writers take a You attitude, they focus on the other person, not on themselves. They highlight the reader's needs, desires, and preferences, not their own. They want to get and keep the reader's attention, and they know that we respond well to people who seem interested in us. Messages from writers who use an I or We point of view sound self-centered and create distance from the reader.

Kim Saleski, a personnel assistant in Gray's Department Store, receives several job applications for a clerk position in the toy department. The store's form asks for a short paragraph describing the applicant's skills and qualifications. When Kim reviews the following two examples, she chooses the writer of the second for a follow-up interview. Why did she make this decision after reading both paragraphs?

Job Candidate 1 – Hosea

I am looking for a job to save money for a car. I know I would enjoy working in your store because I shop there all the time. Another reason I would like to work for your store is that it would help me toward my career goal in marketing. I can come for an interview next week. The following week I'm going on a trip with my friends so next week would be better.

Job Candidate 2 – Marlena

Your job interests me because I have the skills you require. Working with people last summer as a camp counselor gave me experience in communicating with both children and their parents. Also, I volunteer at a local hospital, where I enjoy talking and listening to patients. I know I can serve your customers and would like very much to try. I am available for an interview at your convenience.

Hosea appears more interested in personal concerns than in the needs of the employer. Kim rejected his application immediately. Marlena describes how her background will help the employer, which assures Kim that she understands the importance of a company's profitability.

Follow these guidelines to ensure that your messages center on the reader's needs and not your own.

1. Use positive, You words instead of I words, whenever appropriate, but don't overdo it. You can check yourself by making certain that the You and Your words outnumber the I, We, and My words by at least 4 to 1. Look at how the second example in each set below focuses on the reader.

   - I have enclosed an invoice.
   Your invoice is enclosed.

   - I am happy to enclose a copy of our new vacation policy.
   Your copy of our new vacation policy is enclosed.

   - Our company is pleased to announce the opening of our new store.
   You are invited to attend the gala opening of our new store.

   - I ordered the warehouse inventory software you asked me to get. I'll have it for you in a week.
   Your warehouse inventory software will arrive in a week.

2. Begin messages with words other than I or We.
3. Provide answers to the reader's requests, highlighting information the reader wants to know, and showing how your message affects them.
4. Avoid **negative** *you* words and phrases, such as *you neglected to* or *you failed to.*

You, Your   I
4   to   1

> " Writing when properly managed...is but a different name for conversation. "
>
> — Laurence Sterne

I Want Members

Analyze the following letter for You attitude. How can the letter be improved to highlight the reader's needs? First circle the parts that violate the You attitude, then rewrite the letter correctly.

March 14, 20xx

Centralia Chamber of Commerce
78 Commonwealth Avenue
Centralia, PA 18504

Dear Ms. Lopez:

As the newly elected membership director of the Junior Chamber of Commerce, I am in charge of recruiting new members. I would like very much for you to join. I am working for a record-making membership this year.

We offer a variety of important services, such as Internet connections, 401K plans, health insurance referrals, and monthly get togethers.

I know you'll like the chamber; most of the other young business owners in this town are members and I think you should be also. Fill out the enclosed application blank and return it to me with your check.

Sincerely,

Bob Sandusky
Membership Director, Junior Chamber of Commerce

Activity continued on next page

March 14, 20xx

Centralia Chamber of Commerce
78 Commonwealth Avenue
Centralia, PA 18504

Dear Ms. Lopez:

_____

_____

_____

_____

_____

_____

_____

_____

_____

_____

_____

_____

_____

Sincerely,

Bob Sandusky
Membership Director, Junior Chamber of Commerce

Point Out Reader Benefits

WIIFM, "What's In It For Me?" is a phrase you may have heard. No matter what type of written communication you are preparing, your most important task is to help the reader answer the WIIFM question. How will the reader benefit from granting your request, buying your product, or using your service?

Many of the questions you answered when you analyzed your audience will help you develop a list of reader benefits. If, for example, you are writing a sales flyer for a low-income market, you will focus on low price, value, and extended pay plans; but if you're writing for the high-income market, you may describe the high quality, prestige, or efficiency of your product.

The reader benefit of a vacation home for retirees differs from the benefit of a vacation home for a young couple. Retirees want to hear about convenience, nearby health care, transportation services, entertainment for retirees; and younger couples want to learn about high energy recreational facilities, location of nearby cities, and potential for investment in the property.

The chart below lists examples of documents and their specific reader benefits.

> "Nothing is so simple that it cannot be misunderstood."
>
> —— Jr. Teague

Employee	Document	Benefit to the reader
Salesperson	introduction of new health care insurance	reduce medical premiums by $50 a month
		expanded coverage
Company spokesperson	announcement of a neighborhood cafeteria	nourishing, appetizing low-cost food without tipping
Magazine marketer	invitation to re-subscribe to consumer magazine	25 percent reduction in rate for continuing subscribers

Health Club

As manager of a health club, you plan to write form letters to several different groups of people. You want to customize the letters somewhat by targeting specific benefits for each group. Analyze the readers listed below, then describe the benefit that should be highlighted in each group's letter.

Retirees _____

_____

_____

_____

New mothers _____

_____

_____

_____

Athletes _____

_____

_____

_____

Young, busy professionals _____

_____

_____

_____

Middle-aged executives _____

_____

_____

_____

Be Specific

Rewrite the following sentences to show a specific benefit to the reader. The first example has been completed for you.

1. Our sporting goods store is now located in your neighborhood.

    You are now only five minutes away from the store that can fill all your
    sporting goods needs.

2. You will never regret buying this camera.

    _____

    _____

3. The plastic dinnerware won't scratch or dent, and it won't melt in your dishwasher.

    _____

    _____

4. The odor of this cat food is not offensive.

    _____

    _____

5. We cannot ship your merchandise until July 1.

    _____

    _____

> " The difficulty is not to write, but to write what you mean, not to affect your reader, but to affect him precisely as you wish. "
>
> — Robert Louis Stevenson

GETTING CONNECTED

You can find more suggestions on reaching your audience by logging onto the Internet and visiting the website below.

www.english.uluc.edu/cws/wworkshop/audience.htm

WORKSHOP WRAP-UP

- The most effective messages are written from the reader's point of view.
- Successful workplace writers pay attention to the reader.
- Writing with a You attitude helps focus on the reader's interests, wants, and needs.
- How the reader will benefit from responding to your message needs to be clear and specific.

lbert works as a claims assistant in a state workers' compensation office. His job is to interview claimants who have suffered an illness or injury as a result of their work. Because their employers are legally required to carry workers' compensation insurance, they are eligible for monetary benefits.

Each month he writes a summary and description of the work-related medical problems of the people whom he has interviewed, and identifies those who are eligible to receive benefits. His report is usually very long, and the reading is tedious. Since this report addresses a legal matter, he believes he should include a great deal of detail.

Usually, Albert writes his report in narrative form, sometimes adding last-minute comments to provide further information. Because his work is hectic and he always seems to be in a time bind, he just starts writing and puts in as much as he can find in his notes about each claimant. Albert also includes a list of who is already receiving benefits, the status of their medical condition, how their work is affected by the condition, and the number of new claimants who are eligible for benefits.

Albert's supervisor stops by his office and asks him to make the report more reader-friendly in the future. He comments about the lack of organization, which disturbs Albert.

> **Organization is what you do before you do something, so that when you do it, it's not all mixed up.**
>
> — A.A. Milne

What's Inside

Develop an Organizational Plan

No one likes to hunt for the main point of a business document. In fact, most workplace readers don't have time to read a message twice, so they engage primarily in skimming. They look for the bottom line of the message.

Your letters, memos and e-mail messages and other documents should make the main idea obvious, the back up points easy to find, and the purpose clear, which means that a major portion of your time should be spent planning and organizing what you write. Even employees who don't write often need to know the patterns and formats of clear, well-ordered business documents.

A well-organized document does the following things:

♦ delivers a clear message
♦ uses the reader's time wisely
♦ presents a positive image of the person and the company

Organization of your writing takes practice, but there's no mystery to it. In a well-organized business document, important ideas are easy to locate and easy to understand. If your ideas are out of order and mixed in among several paragraphs, your main message gets lost. When readers have to travel through a maze to find your main point, they may not be able to respond or become so discouraged that they don't continue reading. Send someone an unorganized memo and they may decide that your thinking is unorganized also.

The Basics

Good organization does not change from one type of business document to another. Whether you write an e-mail message, letter, memo, report, or proposal, you should follow the guidelines shown on this page.

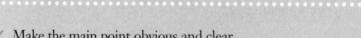

Guidelines for Good Organization

✓ Make the main point obvious and clear.
✓ Check that supporting details relate to the main point and to each other.
✓ Include all important information.
✓ Highlight the main idea and supporting details in an easy-to-follow format.

Incorporate the guidelines in all your business writing. Using these guidelines, Albert can write his report in a clear, coherent manner:

Worker's Compensation Report Contents

Main point	Name, medical condition and employment status of each claimant
Supporting details	The medical condition of each claimant and an expected date for returning to work
Complete information	Details about the employment status and medical condition.
Easy-to-follow format	Single paragraphs about each patient, presented in bullet form or with numbered items

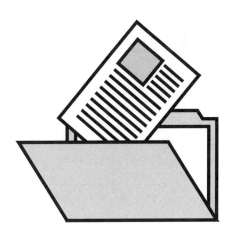

Organize the Words

In the following memo, what is the main point the writer is trying to get across? What are the most important supporting details? Rewrite this memo using three paragraphs. Put the main idea in the first paragraph and backup details in two additional paragraphs.

To: All Employees

From: Marjorie Delaney, Human Resources Department

Date: August 12, 20xx

Subject: New Request Forms

New vacation request forms have been printed with carbon sets of three copies. The yellow copy is to be kept by the supervisor, the pink copy is to be returned to the employee, and the original is to be returned to the Human Resources Department.

All forms must be submitted to the appropriate supervisor by January 15 of each year. Beginning January 1, all requests for vacation must be approved by department supervisors. Requests after the March 10 will not be accepted. Employees should submit their requests to their supervisors, and supervisors will submit their approved requests to the Human Resources Department.

Main Point: _New Vacation Request form (changes)_

Beginning January 1, all requests for vacation must be approved by department supervisors

Supporting Details: _multiple copies_

Additional Supporting Details: _Dates_

Organize Around the Key Points

Jamie works for a company that maintains swimming pools for homeowners. As a pool technician, he knows the steps for organizing his tools and supplies when he goes out on a job. But he's less certain about what to do when he has to write a flyer for customers about a new service the company plans to offer this fall. How should he proceed?

To organize a business document such as a letter, memo, proposal, or report, you must decide what should be included and how the material should be presented. The first task is is plan what you are going to say. Then gather all the information you need and sort through your ideas. Finally, put them in order. These steps usually occur in the following sequence.

> " If you don't know where you're going, you might end up somewhere else. "
>
> — Yogi Berra

Step 1

Identify your reader and the main point

Ask yourself, "Who's going to read this?" "Why am I writing it? Once you figure these out, you are ready to write.

If you're not sure what you want to say, just start writing. You don't have to write the first paragraph first. Once you get beyond the blank page and start getting some sentences down, then you can figure out your main message.

Potential customers are Jamie's readers. His main point is that he wants to tell potential customers about a new winterizing service the company will offer.

Step 2

Provide answers to the reader's questions

Do you have enough details? Imagine your reader is sitting in front of you. What questions would he or she ask? Make sure your document answers your reader's questions completely.

Jamie's readers need to know about cost, timing, materials used, and procedures.

Step 3

Determine a logical sequence

Readers remember information longer and in greater depth when it is presented early in the document. Put your ideas in order of importance. The main idea usually comes first, unless the news is bad, and is followed by supporting ideas of less importance.

Well-organized documents answer readers' questions one paragraph at a time.

Make sure each paragraph pertains to one specific topic and that all sentences relate to that particular topic. Watch out for stray sentences that don't belong.

Jamie's flyer should open with a general paragraph describing the new service and its advantages for customers. Other paragraphs should provide specific details on the procedures used, the materials needed, and the time and costs involved.

Activity 2 gives you practice in identifying the topic and the reader, selecting the backup information, and arranging the details in a logical sequence.

Put These Details in Order

Read the memo below and determine its purpose. Cross out sentences that don't relate to the major topic. Find the sentences that are out of order; then rearrange the entire document so that all points fit together in a logical sequence. As you rewrite the completed message, you may want to adjust some of the wording so that sentences flow together smoothly. Use the chart below the activity to help you revise.

To: All Employees

From: Human Resources Department

Date: January 6, 20xx

Subject: _____(Fill in)

Exercise is great therapy for both the body and the spirit. Remember the yoga class we had three years ago? Please call the exercise coordinator if you have any questions. The woman who taught that class is my next-door neighbor. We want to encourage anyone interested in a total body workout to try these sessions. Join the company's exercise program. In March our exercise program will begin on Monday, March 6, and will continue for six weeks through Thursday, April 20. We'll be doing low impact aerobics, stretching, tightening, and toning. Our instructor, Theresa Bocce, will tailor this program to our wants and needs. Although there is no cost for this program, only a limited number of spaces are available. Please register before February 15.

Who is the reader? _____

What is the main point? _____

What are the most important details that support the main point?_____

Rewrite the memo here:

To: All Employees

From: Human Resources Department

Date: January 6, 20xx

Subject: _____(Fill in)

_____

_____

_____

_____

_____

_____

_____

_____

_____

_____

_____

Write a Good Opening Paragraph

An opening paragraph is like an umbrella, because everything in the document has to fit under it. Opening paragraphs should be general, introduce the topic without going into specific details, and set up the entire document.

No section is more important to the organization of a document than the opening paragraph. Put your readers on the right track in the beginning and they won't get lost later. A clear, informative opening will tell the reader what you're going to talk about and may also suggest how you're going to do it.

Your job as a writer is to guide the readers. Your opening says to the reader, "Here's what I'm going to tell you." A good opening also provides a map for the writer because it is an easy-to-use guide for the full document. In short, an opening paragraph introduces the topic, tells why the topic is important, and helps the reader know what to expect in the rest of the document.

What's Next?

The sample openings shown below from three different letters announce their main topic and preview what's coming up next. Write a sentence that explains what the rest of each memo will contain.

Sample opening 1

Many of you have expressed interest in attending training workshops this year. Thank you for your survey responses telling what you want. This memo explains what the workshops will contain, when they will take place, and how you can sign up.

_____

_____

_____

_____

Sample opening 2

Weather-related cancellations this year have caused the following changes in the calendar.

_____

_____

_____

_____

_____

Sample opening 3

This memo summarizes our conversation on May 2, 20xx and offers three proposals for your consideration.

_____

_____

_____

_____

_____

Show the Reader What's Important

Proper emphasis of ideas can be a serious problem in business writing. Because business writing consists of facts, numbers, and other specific information, it can be technical, dry, and hard to follow. You must highlight main ideas so your writing doesn't become bland and dull.

If you wanted a friend to notice your new car, would you hide it in the garage? If you wanted to show off a new shirt, would you leave it in your closet? Probably not.

Writers get the reader's attention and emphasize key points through a variety of techniques. Although you can't draw stars and circles around the sentences you want to stress, you can use other methods. The list below will help you emphasize the key points of your message.

Emphasizing Key Points

✓ Put the main point in an obvious place, such as in the beginning or in a short paragraph all by itself.

✓ Develop the most important points fully.

✓ Repeat key ideas for emphasis.

✓ Highlight major points with headings and lists.

✓ Use plenty of white space to make your document easy to read. This often means using short paragraphs.

✓ Use italics and bold for emphasis.

> In the long run, men hit only what they aim at.
>
> — Henry David Thoreau

Avoid Organizational Dangers

Most people stay away from danger. They avoid road construction barriers, bare electrical wires, and open manholes. A trouble spot for many inexperienced writers is poor organization. Try to avoid these typical problems.

- *The wastebasket paragraph.* Did you ever read a paragraph more than once, thinking it was your fault because you didn't understand it? Chances are the paragraph had too many details to make any sense.

  These are known as wastebasket paragraphs because everything gets thrown in. Some writers don't take time to get rid of the sentences that don't relate to the main point. They seem to think, "Everything's in there, so let the reader figure out what I mean." When you write, make your revisions before the document goes to the reader.

- *Main point, where are you?* State your main point clearly at the start. People remember best what comes first. The middle of a document or paragraph is a place of less emphasis; therefore, if you hide your central idea in the middle, the reader will have to search for it.

- *The example doesn't fit.* Inexperienced writers sometimes become so pleased with a sentence or paragraph they don't realize it may not fit the message.

  They fall in love with an example and can't leave it out. This is a problem because people don't remember ideas unless they relate to the subject and to each other. After you write a great deal, you will be more comfortable discarding good sentences that don't support the main point.

- *You know what I mean.* Readers are not mind readers. They will not know what you mean unless you tell them. Therefore, you must include enough detail to make your points clear and obvious. Readers pay attention to what you say when you tell them all they need to know.

- *Once upon a time.* Avoid storytelling in business writing. Aside from accident or police reports, most workplace documents do not use a chronological method of organization. For a first draft, you may want to write down information as you think of it or as it happened. But, for your final version, select what's important and arrange the details to support your message.

Review the Do's and Don'ts chart each time you write to make sure you recognize and avoid the signs of poor organization.

Organizational Do's and Don'ts

Do

Use only the essential details.

State the main point clearly at the start.

Write examples that fit the point and relate to each other.

Include enough details to answer all the reader's questions.

Arrange your details in a logical sequence.

Don't

Expect the reader to make your revisions.

Hide your central point in the middle of a paragraph or document.

Fall in love with well-written but irrelevant examples.

Ask the reader to guess what you mean

Tell a story unless the document requires it.

Decide What to Include

Your company will lease or purchase a company car for your use as a computer service technician. Your supervisor has asked you to investigate different options and then to write a memo on the one you recommend. In your investigation you learned a lot about the pros and cons of leasing.

Your notes are filled with information, but jumbled. For example, you found out that leasing long-term may be more economical than short-term, based on the type of vehicle and on other circumstances such as the time of year. You also learned that in comparison to buying a car, someone who leases has a lower monthly cost based on usage.

On the other hand, leasing has real drawbacks like a continuous car payment and higher insurance rates. You are certain your supervisor would appreciate the benefits of driving a new vehicle every three or four years and not have unexpected maintenance fees, but you don't know how he would feel about the limitations of leasing.

Plan how you will organize the material in your report so that it shows what you did and how you arrived at your recommendation. Remember to start with your most important information. Write the memo to your supervisor.

To: Jonathan Willett

From: Your Name

Subject: _____

Date: _____

_____

_____

_____

_____

_____

_____

_____

_____

_____

_____

_____

_____

_____

GETTING CONNECTED

For tips on drafting and organizing many different types of business documents, log on to the Internet and consult "Internet Resources for Business and Technical Writers"

www.english.uluo.edu.cws/wworkshop/ww_tech.html

For general strategies in organizing a document, consult

www.bgru.edu/departments/writing-lab/how_to_effectively_o.html

WORKSHOP WRAP-UP

- Knowing how to organize your writing is an important workplace skill.
- The organizing process includes several steps.
- In most workplace messages, the main point is in the opening paragraph.
- The opening paragraph can set up the organization of the entire document.
- Writers can avoid the problems of poor organization through careful planning.

5 WORKSHOP

Midori works as an adminis–trative assistant in a large health care company. One day her friend Elaine, who sits in the cubicle down the hall, asks for feedback on a document she is drafting for her boss.

As Midori reviews the memo, she finds that it is hard to under-stand because it contains many big words and complex phrases. This surprises Midori because she has always been impressed with Elaine's communication ability.

In one-on-one conversations and when giving presentations, Elaine speaks simply and clearly, using appealing and descriptive words that are easily understandable.

Gently, Midori tells Elaine that the purpose of the message is hidden in all the words. Midori goes on to explain that Elaine should just be herself on paper and use the same words and phrases that she says when she speaks.

Midori describes how writers of some of the best business publications—The *Wall Street Journal* and others—use concise, simple language to express their ideas. She suggests they revise the memo together by following some basic guidelines for effective writing.

What's Inside

In these pages, you will learn to:

> " All writing is a process of elimination. "
>
> —— Martha Albrand

Say What You Mean

Many inexperienced writers think that big words impress readers. The fact is that unnecessarily complex language can be hard to understand. The best business writers communicate their messages in concise, simple language with a positive, businesslike tone.

Today's readers don't have time for stuffy, repetitious phrasings. As you gain more experience reading and writing work-related documents, you will become impatient with writing that's unclear and hard to follow.

Engfish, a term coined by writer and teacher Ken McCrorie describes writing that takes up space but doesn't really say anything. Examine each of the pairs of sentences below to raise your awareness of the need for plain English in business writing. What are the major differences between the A sentences and the B sentences?

Engfish

A We request that you endeavor to locate the communication inasmuch as the manager regards it to be of great importance to today's conference.

B Please find the report because the manager needs it for today's meeting.

A It is the intent of this analysis to take advantage of the basic structure of this type of document to assess the strengths and weaknesses of the communication process within the Taylor Company.

B This analysis will assess the strengths and weaknesses of the communication process in the Taylor Company.

A Managers who are effective give praise to their employees who are outstanding workers and endeavor to implement motivational strategies with subordinates working under them who do not perform well.

B Effective managers praise outstanding workers and try to motivate subordinates to perform at their best.

> " I apologize for writing such a long letter, but I didn't have time to write a short one. "
>
> — Oscar Wilde

Be Concise

Many business people give lip service to the idea that short messages are usually better than long ones. But few writers take the time and trouble to follow this advice. "Keep it short" can become a habit that gets easier with practice. When you realize that many readers skim most of their messages, you will want to make the effort to write briefly and simply. You can turn writing concisely into a game. How can you express your message in the fewest possible words? Can you explain your main point in fifteen words? ten words?

Become a one-page fanatic. Like everything else, practice helps. Look at these two memos about a planned company trip. Which one do you prefer? Why?

Version 1:

Via this correspondence, I wish to inform you that we have been contacted by Eric Harris of the Green Valley Travel Agency concerning the aforementioned trip. We can now release the names of employees who signed up to the tour leader. (40 words)

Version 2:

Eric Harris of the Green Valley Travel Agency has contacted me about the company trip. We can now release the names of interested employees. (24 words)

You probably like the second version better because it's easier to read, shorter, simpler, and more direct. "Via this correspondence" and "I wish to inform you" are extras, words that take up space but do not add any meaning. These are exactly the kinds of phrases you want to eliminate from your writing. Another reason the second version is shorter is it uses the active voice. Later in this workshop, you'll learn how the active voice is clearer and easier to read. You can see from this example that the active voice uses fewer words. For example, "we have been contacted by Eric Harris" is passive voice and uses seven words. The revision in active voice, "Eric Harris has contacted me" is active voice and uses five words. Finally, "aforementioned" and "via" are formal, outdated expressions that take up space and create distance with the reader.

Here are some additional techniques you can use to make your writing concise:

> " The more you say, the less people remember. The fewer the words, the greater the profit. "
>
> — Francois Fenelon

Be Concise

- ✓ Focus on the most important points.
- ✓ Select content carefully: tell only what's necessary.
- ✓ Avoid long sentences.
- ✓ Get rid of phrases and sentences that don't add to your meaning.
- ✓ Get rid of filler words and phrases (*is where, is when; avoid there is*, and *it is* as sentence openers).
- ✓ Use the active voice and action verbs whenever possible.
- ✓ Instead of connecting ideas with "and," show relationships by using words like *because, although, when, while*.

    No: *I got promoted and I'll take you out to dinner.*
    Yes: *Because I got promoted, I'll take you out to dinner.*

- ✓ Use verbs instead of nouns: for example, change -tion and -sion nouns to verbs; instead of saying, we must make a decision, say we must decide; instead of please call if I can be of assistance, say please call if I can assist you.

Simple language is clear, brief, direct, and strong. Be ruthless in cutting out what you don't need. Your readers will thank you and read your messages first!

ACTIVITY 5.1

How Much Can You Cut?

In the example shown below, the revision is 12 words less, still conveys the same message, yet says it more simply and clearly. For the sample activities following the example, keep the same original message but use fewer words. How much can you cut?

Example:

It has been decided that your proposal for an internship is not sufficiently in line with the prescribed qualifications as outlined in the company policy handbook.   (26 words)

Revision:

Your internship proposal does not meet the qualifications outlined in the company policy handbook. (14 words)

Original:

For convenience and coordination, it has been decided that we no longer need separate lists of temporary help for the use of vacation replacements for each separate job in the factory.

Revision:

_____

_____

_____

_____

_____

_____

Original:

In reference to your request of May 3, I am sending you a copy of the article on the job placement process. Supplementary company brochures pertaining to the above-referenced material are also enclosed.

Revision:

_____

_____

_____

_____

_____

_____

_____

_____

Use Simple, Direct Language

Some people today are still holding on to stuffy, overwritten language. Many of these individuals just don't know that they can eliminate jargon and use simple, natural language when they write. Do you recognize any familiar phrases in the list below? Do you see any old friends that you read and write all the time?

Jargon and outdated expressions	Natural, simple expressions
Attached herewith	Enclosed
Prior to	Before
Pending your reply	Until I hear from you
At your earliest convenience	(The date you need a reply)
In regard to	About
At the present time	Now
Wish to say	(This phrase is not needed-just say what you wish to say)
Construct	Build
Interrogate	Ask
Until such time as	When

> **Never use a long word when a short one will do.**
>
> — George Orwell, British novelist

ACTIVITY 5.2

Be Yourself

Substitute natural expressions for the outdated, stuffy language in column 1. When in doubt, ask yourself what you would say to the reader if you were talking over the telephone.

Your old list	Your new list
The undersigned	_____
Initiate	_____
In view of the fact that	_____
Per our conversation	_____
In the event that	_____
Remuneration	_____
Immediate future	_____
Subsequent	_____

Prefer the Active Voice

Business writing experts agree that preferring the active voice is the single most important principle for improving most business writing. Nothing else will do so much so quickly to make your writing readable, concise, and clear.

If you're not sure about the difference between active and passive voice, you're not alone. After you learn how to recognize the passive voice, you can then convert it to the active voice. This process may take time. But it is worth the effort. The fact is that we are all surrounded by the passive voice—inappropriately used. So we're used to reading it and writing it. Let's begin by answering some of the typical questions writers have about the passive voice. That's an important first step to raising awareness.

How can I recognize the passive voice?

You can recognize the passive voice by noting its characteristics:

♦ A form of the verb *to be* (*is, am, are, were, be, been*)

♦ A past participle (a verb ending in *-ed* or *-en* except irregular verbs)

♦ A prepositional phrase beginning with *by* (often missing but understood)

Examples:

Passive:	Five possible solutions to the problem **have been identified** by the project committee.
Active	The project committee **identified** five possible solutions to the problem.
Passive:	A final decision **has been reached.**
Active:	The negotiators **reached** a final decision.

How do I convert passive voice to active?

♦ Make the sentence active by turning the clause around.

Example: When form 135 is received by us, the changes will be made.

When we receive form 135, we will make the changes.

♦ Make the sentence active by changing the verb.

Example: It was felt that the budget was too large.

Many shareholders thought that the budget was too large.

♦ Make the sentence active by rethinking the whole sentence.

Example: The special effects were achieved only after changes in scenery and the sound system.

Changes in scenery and the sound system were important in producing special effects.

> Good writing is one of the two key abilities I focus on when hiring; the other is the ability to read critically. I can train people to do almost anything else, but I don't have time to teach this.
>
> — Richard Todd
> Federal Reserve Bank of Minneapolis

Should I ever use the passive voice? Yes, sometimes it's appropriate, —about 15 percent of the time. The explanations and examples following will help you understand when you may use passive voice effectively.

♦ When you don't know who is doing the acting: *The rebate policy was revoked.*

♦ When the person doing the acting is unimportant to the point you're making: *Many new employees were furloughed.*

♦ When the emphasis is on the person acted upon: *A new CEO was hired.*

♦ When a statement needs to be softened or made impersonal: *Project goals were not reached.*

Here's a summary of all the reasons why you should prefer the active voice:

Passive Voice	Active Voice
wordy	takes fewer words
hard to read	easy to read
often unclear	clear
vague and impersonal	precise
ineffective	strong
omits crucial information as to who did the action	person doing the action is more obvious

> 66 Grammar is a piano
> I play by ear. 99
>
> —— Jean Didion

Make Them Short and Sweet

Show what you learned in the last three sections by rewriting each of the following sentences. Your revisions should be concise, use simple language, and use the active voice wherever appropriate.

1. She will welcome your opinions, and the final decision is to be made by her.

_____

_____

_____

2. After the discussion of project is completed, it is recommended that final report copies be distributed to all project members for their final approval.

_____

_____

_____

3. The results of the survey showed and it was discovered that assigned parking spaces were not appreciated by most of our employees. There are several possible options for increasing space in the employee parking lot after the paving of the old parking lot is completed.

_____

_____

_____

4. This will acknowledge receipt of your memo in which it was mentioned that the report was poorly written and that the boss was not pleased.

_____

_____

_____

5. A meeting was held to define a cost allocation methodology for services provided by the support planning and operations departments.

_____

_____

_____

Adopt a Businesslike Tone

When you're writing to a business associate, you're not writing to a buddy. That means slang expressions and familiar language are inappropriate. If you're ever in doubt about whether the wording of your message may be misunderstood, better take more time to think about what you're trying to say.

Use plain English

Now that you have had some experience in saying what you mean, let's work on revising a draft memo. A memo Jared wrote at his boss' request is shown below.

Techniques we discussed in this chapter, along with some examples taken from the memo are shown in the shaded box.

To: All Staff
From: Jared Williams, Personnel Director
Date: September 10, 20xx
Subject: Designated Areas for the Purpose of Non-staff Personnel Locating a
          Space for Their Cars

It has come to our attention recently that clients, potential customers, and other persons find it difficult to locate an area in which to park their car. Many complaints have been received regarding this matter over the past year. In some cases, people have been tardy for meetings and conferences with our personnel because a place cannot be found for their car.

As a courtesy to all people who visit our facility, please refrain from using non-staff personnel's spaces as areas in which to park your car.

It's easy to use plain English

♦ *Keep it short.* Look carefully at each word to see if it improves the meaning of the document. Eliminate repetitive words that take up space, like *meetings and conferences*, instead of *meetings*.

♦ *Use simple words.* Simple language is more effective than wordy phrases like *non-staff personnel*.

♦ *Get rid of unnecessary expressions.* Several phrases are not needed, like *regarding this matter* and *it has come to our attention*.

♦ *Prefer the active voice.* "Have been received" and "cannot be found" are in the passive voice and can be expressed more effectively in the active voice.

♦ *Adopt a businesslike tone.* Today's readers appreciate language that is upbeat, natural and clear. This memo is overly formal and negative.

Help Elaine Revise

Draft a plain English version for each of the following words, sentences, or paragraphs. All of the examples are taken from Jared's memo on page 58. You may use the suggestions offered in numbers 6 and 7 below. Try to think of the whole document as you revise each word, sentence, or paragraph. When you finish the activity, put the separate pieces together in one, easy-to-read document.

1. tardy   _____

2. refrain   _____

3. people who visit our facility   _____

4. non-staff personnel   _____

5. designated areas for the purpose of non-staff personnel locating a space for their cars

_____

_____

_____

_____

6. Many complaints have been received regarding this matter over the past year. In some cases, people have been tardy for meetings and conferences with our personnel because they cannot find a place for their car.

Over the past year,

_____

_____

_____

_____

7. As a courtesy to all people who visit our facility, please refrain from using non-staff personnel's spaces as areas in which to part your car.

As a courtesy _____, please_____

_____

_____

_____

_____

ACTIVITY 5.4 continued

Write the complete, revised memo here:

    To: All Staff

    From: Jared Williams, Personnel Director

    Subject: _____

_____

_____

_____

_____

_____

_____

_____

_____

_____

_____

_____

_____

_____

_____

_____

_____

_____

_____

Adopt a Positive Approach

You're not surprised, are you, that most people prefer to hear good news than bad news. That makes sense. But we're not talking here about messages that are truly negative, like an employee reprimand or a product cancellation.

Positive communications are important because they build goodwill with readers, help develop a professional image for you and your company, and help you make your work more enjoyable

Most of the messages people send have a positive meaning, "Your request has been granted," or a neutral meaning, "Your payment was received;" but sometimes these messages are presented negatively, and readers respond negatively. For example, look at these pairs:

Note how the last example puts the emphasis on the reader—a good tactic—rather than on the writer

Instead of saying	Our office closes at 5 p.m.
It's just as easy to say	Our office is open until 5 p.m.
Instead of writing	we can't process your order until the necessary paperwork has been completed
You can write	We can process your order when you complete the necessary paperwork
Or, even better	When you complete the necessary paperwork, we can process your order

- Avoid negative expressions, especially ones with the word "you"

I must insist	you failed to	you overlookedyou claim that
you should	I must ask you to	

and words with negative associations:

complain	failure	regret	unfortunately
neglect	inadequate	mistake	

- Use bias-free language. That means avoid language that stereotypes a whole group of people, or presents them in a negative way.

Examples:	Biased:	For a woman, Clarice is a great leader and manager.
	Bias-free:	Clarice is a great leader and manager.
	Biased:	Although sitting in a wheelchair, the new supervisor conducted the meeting.
	Bias-free:	The new supervisor conducted the meeting.
	Biased:	The well-behaved American Indian children waited in line quietly.
	Bias-free:	The well-behaved children waited in line quietly.
	Biased:	The oldsters flocked to the free coffee and donuts at the mall.
	Bias-free:	Many shoppers enjoyed the free coffee and donuts at the mall.

Accentuate the Positive-Eliminate the Negative

Revise each of these examples in positive language.

1. The date of the meeting was listed incorrectly on the brochure.

    _____

    _____

    _____

    _____

    _____

2. It is unfortunate that you have not gotten authorization from your office to attend our training workshop.

    _____

    _____

    _____

    _____

    _____

3. I know that Monday at 2 p.m. is not a convenient time for everyone, but I couldn't find a time that is really good for everyone.

    _____

    _____

    _____

    _____

    _____

4. If you do not show your coupon, you cannot get a reduction in price.

    _____

    _____

    _____

    _____

    _____

GETTING CONNECTED

Individuals who lack confidence in the language forms they use, may log on to the Internet and consult these websites for extra help:

http://composition.cla.umm.edu/CourseWeb/~QkCk/QC_Contents

(includes practice identifying and using the passive voice)

www.Jann.ulue.edu/r~lis/esl/index/html

WORKSHOP WRAP-UP

- The most effective business messages use plain English.
- Short messages are usually easier to read than long ones.
- Writers employ many techniques in writing concisely.
- Simple language is clear, brief, direct, and strong.
- Jargon and outdated expressions take up space and create distance from the reader.
- Preferring the active voice can make your writing readable, concise, and clear.
- Today's readers appreciate language that is upbeat, natural, and clear.

6 WORKSHOP

Richard looks at the report his boss hands him and turns red. It is full of circles, check marks, and changed words. Rick knows that the report probably has misspelled words, grammar errors, incorrect punctuation, and capitalization errors. He is embarrassed that his writing is so poor, and he's finding that it is influencing the way he is seen by his co-workers and his opportunities for promotion.

Once before, he took a community college class to improve his writing skills but gave up when his work load got heavier. The course demonstrated that his writing errors are similar to those made by other business writers.

He has known for some time that he needs to enroll in another class, and this report may be the item that gets him to call the admission office.

Now, though, he has to review the report with his boss. He decides to try to locate some books that can help him with the rewriting. His first book will be be a basic grammar guide that helps him with usage, punctuation and capitalization errors.

What's Inside

> If language is not correct, then what is said is not meant; if what is said is not what is meant, then what must be done remains undone.
>
> — Confucius

Identify Common Errors

What do *you* do when you don't know how to punctuate a sentence, or you can't decide which words to capitalize? How do *you* make decisions about commonly confused words like "affect" and "effect," or "its" and "it's"? Do you try the grammar checker on your computer, consult a printed reference book, ask a colleague, or just yell "Help!" to anyone who will listen?

This *Quick Skills* book will provide some answers to the most commonly asked questions on grammar and mechanics. For other questions, consult grammar hotlines and Web sites, colleagues, your boss, and your own handy pocket guide to correct english.

Handy Pocket Guide to Correct English

Know About Grammar, Usage, and Parallel Structure

Do you know your grammar? Although using correct grammar is not the only key to better writing, it is important to use the correct forms of grammar when writing.

Otherwise, readers may form a negative opinion about your skills. Here are a few basics:

1. Subject/verb agreement

Subject and verb agree in number: a singular subject takes a singular verb and a plural subject takes a plural verb. The subject of a sentence—a new supervisor, a meeting, two invoices—is what you are writing about. These subjects need verbs that match, for example, a new supervisor *is* calling. The meeting and two invoices *are* due.

The number of the subject is not affected by phrases that come between subject and verb.

Singular subjects

Each, every, either, one, another, much, both, few, others, several, anything, anybody, anyone, everyone, someone, nobody, and no one

Plural subjects

All, none, any, some, more, and most may be singular or plural, depending on the noun they refer to.

In the sentence below, changes is a plural subject and takes a plural verb, "are completed."

Changes in the project are almost completed.

2. Pronoun reference

You may recall vaguely the terms "nominative case" and "object of the preposition" from your grammar study. Any time you use a pronoun for a subject, you should use a nominative case pronoun, such as I, we, she, he, they. Just don't use any of these words after a preposition like "to" or "with".

Come to the meeting with John and me. (not I)

Tell my friend and me what you meant.

3. Parallel constructions

Use parallel grammatical constructions to express similar ideas. Parallel constructions are easy to identify and fun to use once you get the hang of them. For example, if you use a list of single words, you shouldn't insert a phrase into the list. If you an "ing" word for the first of your sentence, then you must use an "ing" word for the second part also.

Parallel constructions are especially important in headings and lists.

Wrong:	The new coach is young, personable, and comes with good qualifications.
Right:	The new coach is young, personable, and well-qualified.
Wrong:	Working the telephone system will be easy, but it will be more difficult to respond to customers complaints.
Right:	Working the telephone system will be easy, but responding to customers' complaints will be more difficult.
Wrong:	Joseph enjoys his work as a store clerk during the week and training to become a computer service technician nights and weekends.
Right:	Joseph enjoys working as a store clerk during the week and training to become a computer service technician nights and weekends.

Make The Changes

In the first three pairs of sentences, one is correct and one is not. Place a check mark by the correct sentence. In sentences 4-8, find the errors and correct them in the spaces provided.

1. The new coordinator, Bill, talked with John and me before the meeting.
    I was surprised when Bill asked John and I to chair the committee.

2. My education and experience makes me the best candidate for the job.
    My education and experience make me the best candidate for the job.

3. Jeanne explained her ideas for the workshop, her plans for the daily activities, and why she wanted the project schedule to be revised.

    Jeanne explained her ideas for the workshop, her plans for the daily activities, and her reasons for revising the project schedule.

4. She explained the lesson again for the benefit of Luann and I.

5. The managers will be responsible for planning the new vacation schedule, and they should also implement the new health benefits program.

    _____

    _____

    _____

6. Several employees from the unit winning the prize are going to be congratulated.

    _____

    _____

    _____

7. Your new duties will include answering customers' questions, the supervision of new employees, and you should also plan for the submission of the new budget.

    _____

    _____

    _____

8. The two of us—him and me—decided to apply for the same job.

    _____

    _____

    _____

Choose the Correct Word

Many words in English look alike and sound alike, and that's why they are confusing to many writers. The commonly confused words listed below often cause confusion. How confident are you in using them correctly? Study the pairs in the box, then complete the activity on page 70 to check how many you remember.

Commonly Confused Words

Accept/except [receive/ excluding]	We can **accept** all the files **except** the ones we receive today
Its/it's; you're/ your; they're/ there/their [possession]	**It's** been a long time since I saw the dog look for **its** ball. **You're** invited to the party—don't forget **your** gift. **They're** taking **their** children on a trip. Put the luggage **there**.
you are/ possession they are/adverb, denoting where/ possession]	**"Hers," "yours," "theirs,"** and **"ours"** are written without an apostrophe.
Imply/infer [suggested/ interpret]	She **implied** that she knew him. I **inferred** from her behavior that she didn't.
Bad/badly [adjective/ adverb]	Because of a severe cold, Sally was feeling very **bad**. She behaved **badly** when she heard the news.

Commonly Confused Words continued

Uninterested/ disinterested [lacking interest/ unbiased]	They were chosen to be judges because they were so **disinterested**. Although I had loved the book, I was **uninterested** in seeing the movie.
All ready/ already [as is/previously]	We were **all ready** to leave when she asked us if we had already been given a copy of the agenda.
All right/ alright	Never use **"alright."**
Affect/effect [verb/ noun; both mean influence; also, "effect" can be a verb, meaning to bring about]	The **effect** of wearing seat belts can **affect** the number of people injured in automobile accidents. His administration **effected** many changes in child care legislation.
Farther/further [distance/additional]	We need to discuss that **further**. I don't think I can run any **farther**.
Principle/principal [rule/primary]	The **principal** reason she left the party was that excessive drinking was against her **principles**.
Impact (noun) Impact (verb)	What will be the **impact** of the election on the economy? Don't use the word **impact** as a verb. Avoid: How will the election **impact** the economy?
Lie/lay [rest or recline/ rest or recline]	He **lay** the book on the desk Are you **lying** down because you're tired? Avoid: Are you **laying** down because you're tired?

ACTIVITY 6.2

The Right Word

After reviewing the list of misused words on the previous page, complete the sentences that follow.

1. "I can't go any further," she said, as she limped along on her broken leg.

   _____

2. Are you inferring that you can't complete the project on time?

   _____

3. Which computer is her's? The new employee seems disinterested in getting training on the new software program.

   _____

4. Its' not too early to except invitations to the luncheon.

   _____

5. How will the merger effect your project? Will the company reorganization impact your department?

   _____

6. I feel so badly about his leaving the company.

   _____

7. Did you say your ready to leave for the trip? Alright let's go.

   _____

> Among people with two- or four-year degrees, workers in the top 20 percent of writing ability earn, on average, more than three times as much as workers whose writing falls into the worst 20 percent.
>
> — Stephen Reder, Linguist

Use Punctuation and Capitalization Appropriately

Many people feel overwhelmed by all the punctuation and capitalization rules found in traditional grammar books. Current trends suggest a more open, informal style with fewer marks of punctuation and fewer capital letters. Use punctuation and capitalization to make your message clear and emphatic. Here are some basic rules you should know:

Punctuation rules to remember

♦ **Commas.** Use a comma to show a brief pause. A comma sets off expressions that aren't necessary to the meaning of the sentence **and** separates sentence elements to show how they relate to each other.

Jennifer Thompson, who plans to ask for a transfer, was present at the meeting.
Jennifer Thompson was present at the meeting, but she's planning to ask for a transfer to another department.
Did you know that Bettina Juarez, who is president of New Venture Pictures, will be at the meeting?
Do you know that Bettina Juarez, president of New Ventura Pictures, will be at the meeting?

♦ **Colons.** A colon says "pay attention, something's coming." When you use a colon, you tend to make the second thought in the sentence the most important part.

Colons commonly introduce lists. Generally, you should not use a colon after a verb or preposition.

The order included the following items: paper, software, and tapes.
The order included paper, software, and tapes.
Whoever has the most entries gets a prize: a new car.
We all know why they left early on vacation: they wanted to escape the winter weather.

> I see but one rule: to be clear.
>
> — Stendahl

- **Semicolons.** Use a semicolon to show a strong pause: to link two closely related thoughts not connected by "and" or "but;" to link closely related thoughts connected by *moreover, however, for example, consequently;* and to separate a list or series already containing commas. Look at the examples below.

Example of two closely related thoughts connecting *no, and,* or *but*

The training department held the workshop during the last week in June; many employees could not attend.

Example of two closely related thoughts connected by *moreover, however, for example, consequently*

She canceled the meeting at the last minute; however, two people never got the message.

Example of a series that already contains commas

Three new members were appointed to the committee: Nadia Brilski, representative of the accounting department; Juan Morelli, representative of the technical department; and Bill Atkinson, representative of the administrative team.

- **Dashes.** The dash gives more emphasis than the comma and is a little less formal than the colon. Use the dash to highlight key material and to set up explanatory information in a sentence. Like the colon, the dash points forward to new information. Don't overuse the dash, or you'll lose its effect.

Whoever has the most entries gets a prize—a new car.

I love the Southwest—it has dry weather, gorgeous scenery, and beautiful sunsets.

- **Hyphens.** Hyphens put words together that ordinarily would not be together. If the word is not in the dictionary, then it's two separate words. Generally, if the first word modifies the second, hyphenate.

The long, ten-page report referred to Gisella and me. Between you and me, I was really surprised.

"the long, ten-page report." Ten modifies page, not report.

- **Apostrophes.** Use the apostrophe to show possession and with contractions.

The women's locker room was so crowded that Marie had to put my bag of gym clothes on top of hers.

In today's investment climate, it's almost impossible for a firm to extend credit beyond its regular terms.

Capitalization rules to remember

- Capitalize all official titles when they precede personal names *(Professor Chen)*.
- Do not capitalize occupational titles preceding a name *(instructor Albert Chen)*.
- In general, do not capitalize titles when they follow a personal name *(Albert Chen, chairman of the English Department, Atlantic College)*.
- Capitalize common organizational terms such as *Alphabet Company's Strategic Action Committee* when they are the actual names of units within the writer's own organization, but do not capitalize when they refer to some other organization unless the writer wants to give these terms special importance *(the Strategic Action Committee)*.
- Capitalize such nouns as marketing and purchasing when they are used alone to designate a department within an organization *(the people in Marketing told us...)*
- Capitalize regions of the country but not geographical directions *She lives in the West. After you turn the corner, drive west until you come to the gas station.)*

Add Commas and Capitals

Correct the punctuation and capitalization—and any other errors you find—in this paragraph. First, mark each error, then recopy the paragraph correctly in the space provided.

Denise was employed by kelly manufacturing company several years ago. She started out as a clerk in the accounting department and was their for 6 months before she was transferred to work in the office of the Company President. She used to tell the most interesting stories during lunch. Before she was married she traveled throughout the west even taking a mule trip down the grand canyon. She said she loved to travel each day she had a different story. My favorite was the one she told about her children she had ten girls.

_____

_____

_____

_____

_____

_____

Rules you can forget

You can ignore some of the rules you you learned in the past. Actually, these "rules" were never rules, but many people grew up thinking they were.

1. You **can** end a sentence with a preposition.
    Accepted: *He was the person I had spoken to.*
    Overly formal: *He was the person to whom I had spoken.*

2. You **can** begin a sentence with "and" or "but" or "because."
This "rule" probably came about to help young students write complete sentences and to aid in avoiding sentence fragments.
    Incomplete sentence: *Proofreading can be difficult. Because little time is available to do the job right.*
    Correct: *Proofreading can be difficult. But writers use strategies to find errors.*
    Correct: *Because little time is available to do the job right, proofreading can be difficult.*

Proofread

Do all the interruptions at work make proofreading difficult? Well, proofreading is often very difficult. Even experienced writers tell stories of embarrassing times when an important letter went out with a serious error. But these writers use strategies that minimize the likelihood of sending out documents with incomplete information or obvious mistakes.

Why is proofreading so important? What do you think when you read a letter or report that has sentences missing or words out of order? Most readers conclude that the writer was in a hurry. But the reader may also conclude that the writer didn't know the difference between the correct phrasing and the incorrect one, or even worse, didn't care. That's why errors really do matter. Not because the point of your message won't still get across, but because of the damaging perception you, and possibly your boss, will create in the reader's mind. Here are some strategies that will help you create the right impression:

Proofreading Strategies

✓ *Use your spell checker, but don't depend on it completely.* Remember a spell checker won't distinguish between "in" and "is," or between "form" and "from."

✓ *Read the document out loud.* Mistakes stand out more when read aloud.

✓ *Take a break.* Get up from your desk and get a new perspective. Or put the document aside and work on something else.

✓ *Take your time.* Try not to proofread when you're in a hurry and likely to miss things.

✓ *Find someone else—if possible—to help you check.* Four eyes are better than two for important documents.

✓ *Print on colored paper, in larger type, and double spaced.* Mistakes show up more when they are larger.

✓ *Read the document backwards.* This is a good method for finding mechanical errors.

✓ *Check for one thing at a time.* Picture, if you can, the actual reader and how that person is going to react. Don't try to check spelling at the same time you're reading for meaning and completeness.

✓ *Do it!* Errors detract from your message and undermine your credibility. Allow enough time to proofread carefully and completely.

Find *All* the Errors

The following memo contains many different kinds of errors. As you read, circle the error. Then, in the space below, rewrite the corrected document.

To: All employees
From;   Jenina Miller Project coordinator
Subject: Launching the Millennium Project
Date: October 23, 20xx

It has been announced that are plans for launching the strategic plan ties in closely with the reorganization oft he entire company, however I think the final date will be changed when the new President is hired. Between you and I I'm more optimistic than others about employee support. Each individual will have to do their part in making the transition successful. As you know poor communication costs money wastes time and everyone feels alienated.

Its safe to say that are next project involving team leader Murray Cohen and Gina Ames technology coordinator will be crucial in determining how affective the new millennium project will be.

_____

_____

_____

_____

_____

_____

_____

_____

_____

_____

GETTING CONNECTED

Many Web sites focus on grammar, usage, and the mechanics of punctuation and capitalization. Toll-free grammar hotlines exist in every state with telephone and e-mail information. To access the hotline in your area, log onto the national grammar hotline directory.

www.tc.cc.va.us/writcent/gh/hotlino1.htm

Have you ever been undecided about using "its" or "it's"? Or, "farther" or "further?" Check out the lists of commonly confused words on

http://www.wsu.edu:8080/~brians/errors/errors.html

WORKSHOP WRAP-UP

- Writers can avoid common errors in grammar, usage, and mechanics by identifying the errors and by learning the governing rules.
- Writers find answers to questions on grammar, usage, and mechanical correctness by consulting reference books, grammar hotlines, Web sites, and colleagues at work.
- Business writers use punctuation and capitalization to clarify and emphasize their messages.
- Although correct grammar, usage, and parallel constructions don't—by themselves—guarantee effective writing, business writers need to know and use the correct forms.
- Errors can distract the reader's attention and undermine the writer's credibility.

Leslie loves everything about flowers—their beauty, their wonderful scents, their amazing colors—and she took a job as an assistant in a florist shop just to be around them. When she agreed to do office work for the florist, she never expected she would have to write.

So the first time the owner asks her to draft three documents—a letter to a flower supplier, a promotional flyer about an upcoming sale, and a description of the planned display window for his approval—her mood turns from cheerful to gloomy. She has never felt proficient as a writer, and writing for work really scares her. Although she doesn't want to turn down his request, she hardly knows how to begin.

Leslie calls her friend, Fredrique who works in the next cubicle and asks for help. She expects that Fredrique's job is all about writing and that she will be able to suggest what to write. After she explains her problem, Fredrique says, "Get a good reference guide and follow it. I can't tell you what words to use because you know your business and your customers better than I do. Your documents have to be unique to your business in order to be believable."

She gives Leslie a few pieces of quick advice, "You need to write to the reader's level of understanding, make the most important points early in the letter, be positive, and format the documents so they are easy to read. Just write and rewrite. Patience is what it takes to be a good writer.

Use different formats, depending on the type of document. Good formatting makes your message easier to read."

What's Inside

In these pages, you will learn to:

> " I must write with pains so that my reader may read wtih ease. "
>
> —— Robert Louis Stevenson

Letters

The way written information is presented—its format—has a lot to do with whether it is read and how well it is understood. Choose your formats carefully, use white space, boxes, bullets, and other methods to gain the biggest benefit.

Letters provide a formal or semi-formal way to communicate written information with people outside the company, and memos and e-mail are used for internal written communication. The guidelines below will help you set your letters up professionally.

Use business-style spacing for the parts of letters. The illustration will help you identify the correct number of spaces between the different parts of the letter.

Letterhead (1)	Use business stationery. A professional appearance is important.
Date (2)	Include the month, day, and year.
Inside address (3)	Include the reader's name, title, company, and complete address.
Salutation (4)	Use the standard, Dear *reader's name* spelled correctly. If you don't know the name of the person, try to find out. If this is impossible, use the person's position, like *Dear Service Manager.* Whatever you do, avoid *Dear Sir or Madam* because it is stilted and old-fashioned.
Body of letter (5)	Contents of letter.
Closing (6)	*Sincerely* is the standard closing.
Writer's signature (7)	Include the writer's name and position typed below the signature.

Welkley Business School
203 Lancaster Avenue
Wayne, PA 19087 (1)

May 4, 20xx (2)

Sandra Gonzales
English Department
Harvey High School (3)
399 St. Clair Street
Winfield, IL, 60190

Dear Ms. Gonzales: (4)

Thank you for asking about block style letters. (5)

Block-style letters are popular because they are so easy to type. Every line begins at
the left margin.

Since this letter is typed on letterhead stationery, there is no heading. If it had been
typed on plain stationery, the heading would begin at the left margin.

This letter illustrates closed punctuation; which means a colon follows the salutation
and a comma follows the closing. Four spaces follow the date line. Additional spaces
can be added to make shorter letters more attractive.

Do you agree that the block style letter has a clean, modern appearance?

Sincerely, (6)

Patricia Kendall (7)
Department of Communications

Finish This Letter, Please

Revise, key and print the letter shown below. Make certain that your final version is neatly typed and is easy to read. Make up a letterhead and address and any other information you believe you need.

- Start with the sentence that sums up the purpose of the letter.

- Reorganize the letter into several paragraphs with the details that back up the main point. Imagine yourself receiving and reading this letter. What details would encourage you to sign up for a trip?

- Build goodwill. Make the last sentence friendlier.

- Name the bus company and manager.

- Be concise. Readers get lost in repetitive sentences.

- Write from the reader's point of view. Use you-centered language. For example, change *we have new places to go* to *you can visit new places.*

Dear Bus Patrons:

Enclosed please find reservation forms and a complete schedule of trips for our 20xx season. Our bus fleet has expanded and we changed many of our schedules. We have new places to go, some new overnight trips, and a chance to see an excellent musical in Central City. We expect to have an even bigger and better season than last year.

America's Tours is planning an exciting spring, summer, and fall season. We plan to visit the Berson Gardens, the new Design Museum in Pepperton, and the historic Kellogg House.

Our most popular trip—fall foliage in the Endless Mountains—is usually reserved well in advance. If you would like to schedule a day or overnight trip for your club or organization, or for yourself, you MUST make a reservation. It is not possible to hold a particular date without the required paper work.

Also, we had to replace two malfunctioning vehicles this year with brand-new comfortable buses. You're going to love them. They have wider seats, softer cushions, and more leg room.

We expect a great season this year and hope you'll join us. Please call me if you had any complaints about last year's trips. Or if you have any special requests.

Sincerely,

Memos

Often, memos are replaced by e-mail messages because of speed of delivery, but they continue to be used by many writers. Unlike many letters, memos have a subject line but no salutation or complimentary closing. Both letters and memos can be of any length, serious or casual, simple or complex.

Follow the same pattern for writing a memo that you would for any informative message. Note the memo format in this example:

To: Operations Department Staff

From: Bonita Crowell, Operations Manager

Date: May 3, 20xx

Subject: Preferences for Summer Vacation

Taking good care of all of our customers is our first priority this summer. That means our office will remain open and functional at all times.

So that we keep both our customers and employees happy, vacations need to be scheduled early so that all time periods are staffed adequately.

Please let me know your vacation preferences in priority order. The sooner I receive your requests, the sooner I can develop a fair and satisfactory schedule.

Thanks.

Subject Lines

How do you feel when you face a computer screen filled with endless subject lines of e-mail messages? Do you like to read a long, difficult memo with a vague subject line at the end of a busy day? Most business readers appreciate subject lines that are short, clear, and easy to read.

Both memos and e-mail messages employ subject lines. Like titles, subject lines are important because they present the first chance to get your message across to the reader. Subject lines do the following:

♦ tell readers the reasons for reading the document
♦ assist in filing or retrieving a document

The best subject lines are specific, informative, and concise.

Subject Line Guides

Specific.   Subject lines need to be specific enough to differentiate a document from others on the same topic.

Original: Maintenance Budget, 1999-2000
Revision: Request for New Items in Maintenance Budget, 1999-20xx

Informative.   Sum up neutral news, tell good news, avoid bad news in subject lines.

Neutral: Budget Meeting Rescheduled
Good: Invitation to Company Picnic
Bad news
avoided: Changes in Product Cycle (*changes will mean more work for everyone*)

Concise.   Avoid long noun strings that are hard to read.

Original: Employees' Work Schedule Preferences Results Reported
Revision: What Employees Like and Dislike about Their Work Schedules

> Writing is one of the easiest things; erasing is one of the hardest.
>
> — Rabbi Israel Salanter

Be Specific

Revise each of the following subject lines according to the guidelines on the previous page. You may have to add material of your own to subject lines that are too general.

1. Presentation Critique

_____

_____

_____

_____

_____

_____

2. Vendor Bidding Software Inputting Information

_____

_____

_____

_____

_____

_____

3. Employee Layoffs

_____

_____

_____

_____

_____

_____

New Opportunities Available

Write a memo to all staff members announcing a new round of teamwork training workshops and inviting their participation. Key and print the memo in proper form.

To: All Staff

From: Belinda Cho, Operations Office

Subject:

_____

_____

_____

_____

_____

_____

_____

_____

_____

_____

_____

_____

_____

_____

_____

_____

_____

_____

_____

_____

_____

_____

E-mail Messages

E-mail, or *electronic mail*, fulfills a very important function in today's business world. But be careful, e-mail often becomes overused and misused.

Using e-mail properly is an essential skill for everyone. The writing principles are the same as for a letter or memo, but the format depends on your specific Internet service. Most e-mail messages are written in a straight-forward paragraph format. When it's possible to use bullets or other formatting techniques, do so to enhance the readability of your message.

Here are some basic tips to remember:

♦ Proofread your e-mail carefully; apply all you know about good writing techniques.

Just because e-mail is informal doesn't mean that you can risk grammatical and typographical errors.

♦ E-mail is not private. Others may copy your messages and send them to individuals you didn't write to. Recognize that your employer can check your e-mail. Be sensible and careful in what you write.

♦ Handle conflict in person, if possible, rather than by e-mail. Written messages can be more readily misunderstood and live on even after the matter has been settled.

♦ Try to keep your system of sending e-mail copies simple and sensible. Don't send copies of messages to people unless requested.

♦ In order to cope with message overload, many companies label all messages as either *informational* or *action items*, in order to avoid wasting time.

> "The difference between the right word and the almost right word is the difference between lightning and the lightning bug."
>
> — Mark Twain

E-mail Messages

Compose an e-mail message to relay the following information. Include other points you think are important. Use your own wording in the e-mail message.

An individual from company headquarters will visit the plant in a few days to investigate whether all safety regulations are being followed. Everyone should inspect their work areas thoroughly and report possible problems immediately.

To: All Staff

From: Moesha Bell, Operations Department

Subject:

_____

_____

_____

_____

_____

_____

_____

_____

_____

_____

_____

_____

_____

> I'm exhausted. I spent all morning putting in a comma and all afternoon taking it out.
>
> — Oscar Wilde

Short Reports

Entry-level employees often have to write short reports: summaries of meetings they've attended, results of a survey their boss conducted, a description of a machine malfunction. Short reports utilize all the principles of clear organization and simple, plain English. They are informative in nature and use the memo format, although they are usually longer than routine memos. Revise, key and print the short report below so that Maria can rationalize her new computer.

ACTIVITY 7.5

To: The Technology Services

From: Maria Sanelez

Subject line: _____

During the summer I began having problems with my Sage computer. The computer was taking quite a while to initialize itself in the morning when it was turned on. Initialization is normally immediate, however, it was now taking approximately five minutes. As the summer progressed, I began having problems when I saved a document and then tried to print it. The hard drive was having trouble locating the file that had just been saved so that it could be printed.

I notified Yangley Romaine of the computer problems I was having and she called for service. The serviceman checked over the computer and said the problem appeared to be with hard drive. It was having trouble retrieving data. He reinstalled my software explaining that sometimes this will help increase data retrieval. The computer appeared to function satisfactorily for a few days, but the problems with initialization began to appear again.

Over the next few weeks, the problem became progressively worse. Every time I tried to print a document, the hard drive would have trouble retrieving the data. It would take several tries before the computer would find the data and print it. On one occasion, after my tenth try at trying to print my document, the hard drive automatically shut itself down. I rebooted the system. When the menu came up, I made one selection, and the system immediately went into a general failure and printed the following message on the screen: Abort, Retry, Ignore.

I selected Retry and the menu appeared on the screen. I tried print and the hard drive again tried to retrieve my data to print it. After several tries the hard drive shut down. I rebooted the system, selected from the menu, and the system immediately went into general failure again. I continued through this process several more times, but no luck. I turned off the computer, very discouraged.

The next day I turned the computer on and went through the same procedure of general failures and having to reboot the system. On my final attempt of trying to retrieve my data, I got a long error message. The serviceman was called, and in going over my computer, said it showed signs of hard drive failure. The hard drive should be replaced.

At the present time, I have a Sage model 3 computer sitting on my workstation that does not function at all. I have had to impose on my work colleagues to use their computers so that I can complete my work. But that doesn't work because they have to use their computers and I have to wait around and waste time that I could be using on a computer.

GETTING CONNECTED

Are you every puzzled by e-mail etiquette? You can find out the latest on e-mail etiquette by logging onto

www.etiquette.net/index.html

For more information on formats for memos, cover letters, and reports, log on to

www.rpi.edu/dept/llcwritecenter/web/handouts.html

WORKSHOP WRAP-UP

- Workplace documents come in various formats: letters, memos, e-mail and short reports, as well as newsletters, proposals, brochures, policy statements, instruction manuals.
- The standard block letter format is one of the most commonly used business documents.
- Like letters, memos can be long or short, serious or casual, simple or complex.
- E-mail users employ techniques to use this type of communication productively.
- The subject lines are specific, informative, and concise.
- Short reports fulfill various functions: they summarize, describe, explain, and convey information.

Checklist for Workplace Writing

✓ Focus on the reader in every document you write.

✓ Identify the purpose in every document you write.

✓ Write messages with an obvious You attitude.

✓ Show clear benefits to the reader.

✓ Organize your documents around the key points.

✓ Use opening paragraphs that set up the organization of the entire document.

✓ Put the main point up front.

✓ Supply the relevant details.

✓ Close on a positive note.

✓ Begin negative messages with a neutral or positive or buffer statement.

✓ Give the reason for a refusal.

✓ State or imply the refusal.

✓ In a request message, clearly state the action you want.

✓ Begin a persuasive message with a startling statement or a question.

✓ Use a strong, goodwill closing.

✓ Make the most of goodwill messages to enhance your business relationships.

✓ Show the reader what's important with headings, lists, and white space.

✓ Avoid organizational dangers like wastebasket paragraphs and chronological storytelling.

✓ Use enough details to answer all the reader's questions.

✓ Avoid excessive jargon and outdated expressions.

✓ Write concisely.

✓ Use language that is upbeat, natural, and businesslike.

✓ Use the active voice and action verbs whenever possible.

✓ Develop a positive tone in all your writing.

✓ Proofread all your documents carefully for errors in grammar and mechanics.

✓ Follow the rules for correct punctuation and capitalization to add clarity and emphasis.

✓ Identify and use parallel constructions in your writing.

✓ Use online resources to find the answers to your grammar questions.

✓ Use the standard block format in business letters.

✓ Write clear and concise memos.

✓ Write specific, informative, and concise subject lines.

✓ Organize short reports so that the main points stand out in an easy-to-read format.

Revising Guidelines

Use this checklist to help you revise your documents to add clarity, completeness, and correctness.

Step 1: Content and meaning

Is the purpose stated clearly?

Is all information accurate?

Are all essential details included?

Step 2: Structure

Is the main idea up front?

Is the document organized around what the reader needs to know?

Do headings and bullets highlight key information?

Step 3: Paragraphs and sentences

Are paragraphs short—5-6 lines—with one major idea?

Are both long and short sentences used for variety?

Step 4: Tone and style

Is the language simple and concise?

Is the tone upbeat and positive?

Step 5: Grammar and mechanics

Are typographical errors corrected?

Are spelling, punctuation, and capitalization accurate?

Are grammar and usage correct?

Step 6: Overall

Is the document clear, correct, complete, and easy-to-read?

Also in the
QUICK SKILLS SERIES

Attitude and Self-Esteem

Listening

Reading in the Workplace

Self-Management and Goal Setting

Speaking and Presenting

Decision Making and Problem Solving

For information on new titles:
call 1-800-354-9706
or visit us on-line at
www.swep.com